BUREAUCRATS HOW TO ANNOY THEM!

R. T. FISHALL

Drawings by William Rushton

SIDGWICK & JACKSON
LONDON

To all bureaucrats and Civil Servants, everywhere. If this book makes your lives even the tiniest bit more difficult, it will have been well worth writing.

First published in 1981 in Great Britain by
Sidgwick and Jackson Limited.

ISBN 0-283-98785-5

Printed in Great Britain by A. Wheaton & Co., Ltd., Exeter

for Sidgwick and Jackson Limited
1 Tavistock Chambers, Bloomsbury Way
London WC1A 2SG

CONTENTS

BUREAUCRATS
*HOW TO
ANNOY THEM!*

Introduction:
Or, the
Gas Bill
Cometh

One glorious spring morning, when the birds were singing happily in the tree-tops and from my rose garden I could hear the waves murmuring softly in the distance, I had a Final Demand from the Southern Gas Company. It was signed by a Mr K. Whitmarsh, and was quite uncompromising. Either I immediately paid a £10 bill for repairs to the central heating system in my house, or else I would be prosecuted with the full rigour of the Law.

Since my central heating system is powered entirely by oil, the situation was fraught with interest at once. Rather wanting to see what would happen, I sent a cheque for £10, with a letter of inquiry. The results were remarkable. I had, on successive days:

1   A letter from Mr Whitmarsh, saying that I probably didn't owe the £10.

2   A second letter from Mr Whitmarsh, saying that I certainly didn't owe the £10.

3   A refund of my £10.

4   A second refund of the same £10.

5   A second Final Demand.

This struck me as being rather curious, and I began making investigations far and wide. Evidently quite a number of people had heard from Mr Whitmarsh in the same vein, some justifiably and others not. I christened him Twitmarsh, a name by which he is still generally, if not affectionately, remembered.

All in all, it set me thinking. What if Mr Twitmarsh's letter had landed on the doorstep of an old age pensioner of modest means and nervous disposition? And anyway, why should the great British public be pushed around by Twitmarsh or any other Twitmarshes? We are not ruled directly by Parliament, but by minor officials — bureaucrats of all descriptions, safely embraced in the arms of the Civil Service, with immunity from dismissal and nice, inflation-proof pensions. Unfortunately they hold all the cards, particularly since they can always retire behind a cloak of anonymity if things get really hot.

Of course, there are exceptions. Do you remember the Crichel Down scandal of more than a quarter of a century ago? An open piece of legal skulduggery, involving the compulsory purchase of land belonging to one Commander Marten and its subsequent sale by the Civil Service at a vast profit, was taken to the highest levels, and led to the eventual resignation of the minister concerned, whose name I forget. But not everyone has the courage, the skill, or — more importantly — the financial resources of Commander Marten, and lesser mortals have no choice but to give in meekly.

Unless, of course, we can do something about it.

I thought that Twitmarsh must have been in a class of his own so far as the Gas Board was concerned. But not so! A year later (actually, in 1979) I had a brusque Final Demand from the North Thames Gas Company. This time it was for £865.47, and concerned the installation of gas central heating in a building in Lowndes Street, S.W.1. Again I was baffled. The letter was signed not by Mr Twitmarsh (who had moved on to higher things, and wasn't in the North Thames orbit anyway), but by a Mr W. Bonney.

I could have played it gently, and upon reflection I wish I had. In fact, I admit that for once in my life I became cross. My letter back began: 'Dear Mr Bonney: I realize that Gas Board officials are notoriously thick as well as rude, but for sheer dithering incompetence your letter is unrivalled in my experience.' I continued along the same lines, pointing out that I had never heard of Lowndes Street, and that the entire gas supply in my country home consisted of a small stove upon which I occasionally boil a kettle.

I then telephoned, and elicited some useful information. Fortunately I was put through to a junior clerk, who was not accustomed to such contretemps, and who blurted out the whole story. First, although the letter was signed 'W. Bonney', not 'p.p. W. Bonney', it was not Mr Bonney who had signed it; he was away on sick leave, and the signature had been written by a Miss Whitty in the same department. There really was someone of my name in Lowndes Street, and he did owe £865.47, but it wasn't me. Not being sure whom to

chase, Miss Whitty had consulted the current edition of *Who's Who,* looked up the first person of that name — who happened to be me — and launched her Final Demand...

The next person I contacted was Mr Gadd, the Chairman of North Thames Gas. After considerable difficulty I got through to him on the telephone, and put him abreast of the situation. The next part of the conversation went like this:

ME. *Well, what is the explanation?*

MR GADD. It was a mistake in our computer department. It was an administrative slip-up by a senior employee.

ME. *Oh, no, it wasn't. It was a slip-up by your Miss Whitty. Didn't you know?*

MR GADD. Gulp.

Further researches showed me that the real owner of the Lowndes Street premises had departed for Spain. I last heard of him in Madrid, and whether Mr Gadd and Miss Whitty ever caught up with him I do not (yet) know. But there are several much more serious aspects of the whole episode.

An O.A.P. receiving a threatening demand of that kind would possibly have a heart attack. I was not in the least alarmed — but I am not of a nervous disposition, I am not an O.A.P., and I am not penniless. As soon as my initial annoyance had passed, I could see the funny side of it. But the clanger was even worse than Twit-marsh's, and if it is typical (as may well be the case) then something ought to be done. Moreover, how did Miss Whitty come to sign the letter 'W. Bonney'? Signing other people's names without a 'per pro' is not exactly within the law, and even Mr Gadd could not deny that this was what Miss Whitty had done. (Whether he would have told me had I not found it out independently, it is not for me to say!)

Somehow or other, Gas Boards always seem to be edging their way into the news. During the early autumn of 1980, for instance, Southern Gas put up a truly superb performance at Emsworth in Hampshire, a pleasant little village near the coast. Their workmen dug a large hole, twenty-five feet across, on the west side of one of the main streets, and left it there, ostensibly because they were laying a new main. Nothing more happened for over a month, and since the hole was right in the middle of the main shopping area all pedestrians had to thread their way around it. Presently it became a sort of rubbish dump, and was filled with miscellaneous bric-à-brac, together with weeds sprouting in all directions. People complained, but the Gas Board remained silent. Mr Mike Hewish, director of a house furnishing firm, was particularly badly off, since the hole was slap in his way. He persisted in his inquiries, but with no result. Mr Hewish then fell into the hole. After another month, a Gas Board spokesman explained that the two workmen assigned to the task had been away on sick leave.

Note that the statement was issued by 'a spokesman'. These gentlemen always prefer to stay strictly in the background, and it should be the public's task to ferret them out. Gas Boards in general are, it seems, a haven for Twitmarshes. Moreover, in a country with over two million unemployed, it seems a little strange that the local officials were unable to find two other people competent to fill in a hole. Remember, gas prices have risen out of all belief during the past year or two.

Not that Gas Boards are alone. Electricity Boards have their Twitmarshes too. They have a delightful little habit of sending deliberately inflated bills to O.A.P.s who haven't paid up promptly, the idea being that it will frighten them – and it does. (We have here a symptom of the unpleasant species known as the Bureaukraut, of whom more anon.)

Next, consider the Post Office Telephone Service. These Twitmarshes send out bills which cannot possibly be checked, so the luckless subscriber has no option but to take the demands on trust, which is always a dangerous thing to do. When one can make a firm check, it is often found that the demands are a good deal too high, but checks are now becoming more and more difficult to make – the G.P.O. sees to that, not because of deliberate chiselling, but because Post Office officials depend entirely upon computers, and can't be bothered to work things out for themselves.

Neither are telephone men invariably co-operative. For instance, in October 1980 (again!), an elderly and frail couple in Southbourne, Mr and Mrs Thompson, asked for the faulty cable to their bedside telephone to be repaired. In mending the fault, the Post Office engineer shortened the cable, so that the telephone came to rest on the far side of the room, and Mr and Mrs Thompson had to climb out of bed to answer it. When they complained, the inevitable spokesman said that the house was registered for one telephone only, so nothing could be done. Under the circumstances, it was rather odd that the Thompsons had been paying rental for two telephones for several years...

There is, of course, an Ombudsman, whose duties are to protect the public from unfair dealing by Twitmarshes and other officials. It is fair to say that the Ombudsman has as much real power as a raspberry blancmange, and even when he comes down in favour of the victim (as he often does), nothing ever happens.

Let me repeat that the Twitmarshes hold all the aces, as well as the kings, and most of the queens as well. The general public has no conventional redress. Which means that other methods must be adopted, and must remain strictly within the law.

The method I propose, therefore, is quite simple:

MAKE THE BRUTES WORK.

The present slim volume is a preliminary study only. But, as I have said in the Dedication, if it makes the lives of Twitmarshes even the tiniest bit more difficult, it will have more than served its purpose.

B - B

Fundamental
Laws

First, then, let us list some important principles, which will, if sufficiently widely followed, make an encouraging start to the campaign. To this end I have compiled a set of Fundamental Laws (F.L.s), though these must be taken as generalizations only. But at the outset there is one very important and very serious qualification to be made. *None of the Laws should ever be applied except where Twitmarshes are concerned.* I have not the slightest sympathy for a man who owes, say, a £10 bill to the local baker, and doesn't pay it on the nail. This is basic honesty, and anyone who does not agree is not on my wavelength at all.

Here, then, are the Fundamental Laws.

---

1   When writing to a Twitmarsh, never be explicit. Word your letter in such a way that it can mean almost anything.

---

2   In general, write it instead of typing it. Make it long, verbose and only semi-legible.

---

3   Make what you can of signatures. I remember a letter from a tax inspector whose signature was merely a squiggle. It looked to me like Mc-Hedgehog, but to use an obviously improbable name does not have the desired effect, so twist

it as judiciously as you can. For instance, if the actual name of the Twitmarsh is W. Harris (*[signature]*), write back to W. Hammond.

---

4   Never give a correct reference. If, for instance, you have a letter from the Tax Office with reference EH/4/PNG/H8, head your letter back either WS/3/JGH/H9 or, if you prefer, nothing at all. But always give a reference of your own; this may come in useful later, because –

---

5   It is often a good idea to request a reply to a letter that hasn't actually been written. If you ask for a prompt response to your letter of 6 August, reference ED/8/GF.27, and your last genuine letter has been referenced ED/8/GF.26, you will force the Twitmarsh to waste much time in searching for a letter that has never existed. (Obviously bogus references, such as BA/LLS, may give a certain amount of personal satisfaction, but they are not really useful. My advice is to avoid them.)

---

6   In paying a bill, for instance to the Inland Revenue, never make it out for quite the right amount. Write

it slightly but just significantly wrong, as there is nothing better calculated than this to sugar up a computer. It doesn't matter whether you send just too much, or just too little; if the former, you can start an interminable correspondence to reclaim it, or deduct an equivalent amount from your next cheque, again perceptibly wrong. A discrepancy of a few pence is not enough, and a discrepancy of more than a pound or two is too much, because it may give the Twitmarsh a lever which he can use (assuming that the bill has been underpaid). In general, I recommend a discrepancy of between 50p and £1.75.

---

7   A well-placed staple in the middle of a cheque, attaching it to the accompanying letter (see illustration) has been known to jam a computer completely. It is therefore worth trying.

---

8   Dates on letters to Twitmarshes should always be slightly wrong. But remember to keep accurate notes of the correct dates, because you may need them at any time.

---

9   Never pay a tax bill, rates demand, etc., without making sure that the Twitmarsh concerned is

forced to write at least half a dozen unnecessary letters. I will enlarge upon this later. My present record is seventeen.

---

10 Stamps must always be affixed to letters to Twitmarshes of course, as anything else is illegal. However, there are people who omit the stamp and put 'Official' on the upper right-hand corner of the envelope when a Twitmarsh fails to send a stamped addressed envelope.

The placing of a stamp is also something to be considered. Generally, put it in the left-hand corner instead of the right. There was one case in Tunbridge Wells, years ago, of a man who went a step further, and when writing to the taxman or the local council always put his stamp in the exact centre of the envelope. Finally the G.P.O. lost patience, and sent the offender a letter asking him to be more conventional in future. By return, the Head Postmaster received a letter, with the stamp in the centre, as before. When he opened the envelope, he found a brief but relevant verse:

> *Hey diddle diddle,*
> *The stamp's in the middle.*

---

11 Always file your correspondence with the utmost care. Nothing daunts a Twitmarsh more than to be

confronted with an accurate quote either from a letter of his or from one of yours, dating back several years. Naturally, the same applies to bills and receipts — and here, I am afraid, bureaucrats are not unique. I can cite a case in point. I had paid a trader's bill (let me add that it was not in my present home village; it happened a long time ago now). Months later I had a second bill for the same amount and the same goods. As I had filed the receipt, I was safe; but I found out later that that particular trader was somewhat financially embarrassed, and had told his clerk to send out repeats of all the last quarter's accounts — and more than 60 per cent of his customers paid up in all innocence! Fortunately, however, these episodes are rare in private trading, and do not come within the scope of the present study.

When sending back a completed V.A.T. or tax form (filled in, of course, according to the above F.L.s), a very important gambit is to crumple it, then smooth it out and re-fold it. I am assured that there is nothing better than a crumpled form to jam up any Twitmarsh's computer!

Having cleared the air, so to speak, let us now turn to some specific problems.

The
Inland
Revenue

There can be no doubt that to most people the chief enemy is the income tax inspector. To him all the F.L.s should be rigorously and continuously applied.

The impression the Inland Revenue tries to give is that of a service staffed by kindly, conscientious, basically decent officials who are doing their job in a thoroughly efficient way, and who are always ready to help and advise. This may be true in some cases — I have no doubt that it is. Alas, it is not universal, and one sometimes encounters a real maggot.

V.A.T. men have the reputation of being the nastiest of the lot, and they can go to incredible lengths. Consider, for instance, the case of Mr James Shinner, publican of The Sportsman in St John's Precinct, Liverpool. One day in April 1980 he gave no more than a cursory glance at a man who was showing a keen interest in the chips and peas on the plate in front of him. Horrors! A careful count showed the diner that there were exactly thirty chips on the plate, each two inches long by a quarter of an inch square. Counting the peas came next; there were seventy of them. Back at his headquarters, he passed on this valuable information to a colleague, who took a potato and cut it into thirty chips, two inches long by a quarter of an inch square, weighed them, and arrived at a total of four ounces. As a result of this research, the Customs and Excise decided that Mr Shinner owed an extra £746.93 in V.A.T.

This, believe it or not, is absolutely true.* Unfortunately — and I stress this again — the tax inspector is in an almost unassailable position. He need not divulge his sources of information, even when they are blatantly wrong; he is protected by the full majesty of the law; and even if he is caught out — well, what does he care? It isn't his own money that is at stake, and the very worst that can happen is that he receives a gentle reprimand from the Ombudsman or some equally futile source, which can be read with an amused sneer and then consigned to the waste-paper basket. In fact, by making excessive demands, he has everything to gain (promotion?) and nothing to lose. In general his victims come from those who have no effective defences: authors, artists, actors, freelances of all kinds — those who depend upon themselves rather than upon Trade Unions, and who are thus ideal subjects for milking.

It is, then, absolutely essential to keep within the strictest bounds of legality all the time, and to take the greatest care that no loop-holes are left into which the tax man can thrust his grubby paw.

To enlist the services of a tax avoidance expert (note that I say tax avoidance, not tax evasion, which is a completely different thing) costs a great deal, and the returns may or may not be worthwhile. Obviously, the freelance will be wise to do it if he can, but not being anything of an authority in these matters myself I do not consider myself competent to say more.

---

*It has been reported that one V.A.T. man engaged in a similar errand was spotted in time, and was given soup containing a powerful laxative. But this may be apocryphal, and is in any case against the law. . .

Frankly, though, the people of Britain would be much less averse to paying taxes if they were sure that their money would not be poured down the bureaucratic drain. Civil servants increase in number every week — and there is another point to be made also. Not long ago (1980) the Government bequeathed £50 million to Sri Lanka to build a bridge, entirely without strings attached to the gift; another £50 million to Nepal for something of the same kind, and £70 million as a first gift to the new government of Zimbabwe. I wonder how many kidney machines could have been bought with that money, for the benefit of people in our own country who are dying and cannot be properly cared for?

However, I digress.

We must adopt the most basic of all principles: *Make the brutes work.* Begin, then, by questioning the amount of tax demanded. When the reply comes, write back (following the F.L.s laid down earlier, of course), and put some entirely irrelevant query which sounds plausible even though it isn't. For example:

I was under the impression that my car allowance had been carried over from last year, because as I told you in my letter of 8 September (ref. GDS/45/ Q.2) I have been compelled to buy a new vehicle; my old one had developed brake trouble, and I am afraid that there was also an unacceptable amount of rust on the chassis, which meant that there was an ever-increasing danger of mechanical failure, which was the main subject of my earlier letters, to which you replied (ref. YSD/W/76.S2) stating that there were regulations dealing with the amounts of allowances concerning vehicular maintenance in general, and which I interpreted as being applicable in my own case, particularly since I had used my old car ever since I bought it some years ago — it has given me good service, and I cannot complain; it was, as you know, a Volvo — and when considering the purchase of a new one, I naturally had to take all tax eventualities into account, which is why I originally wrote to you last 19 January asking whether there were any additional circumstances which could be applicable in this and similar cases, though of course I did not realize that the allowances were not payable over a period of time, and that the actual purchase of a new vehicle, particularly one with a V registration which I obtained second-hand at a price which I consider reasonable, was only a part of the considerations which you would feel able to take into account. I make the allowance £40. Is this right, please?

If you have paved the way by sending a previous letter (or letters), all to the good. And if you write in longhand, it will be calculated to make the Twitmarsh scratch his head in a mournful manner and reach wearily for the nearest gin and tonic.

His reply is likely to be quite short. Leave things for a few days, and then send a xeroxed copy of exactly the same letter, marked 'Copy of letter sent on 1 July' — you needn't say that it has already been answered, and the Twitmarsh will have no real option but to plough through it again. This process can be suitably extended in many ways, and can be a valuable gambit.

Tax forms, of course, are made deliberately complicated. One procedure that I have followed several times is to send back a form of my own, thus:

To the Income Tax Inspector,
Lower Bassington-on-the-Ribble.

Dear Sir,

For my records (ref. GH/54/GNR.2) I require the following information, which should be provided at your earliest convenience.

(a) Name of tax office _____

(b) Full address _____

_____

(c) Tax paid to end of last financial year (198) _____

(d) References to forms upon which tax was based _____

(e) Allowances deducted _____

(f) References to allowance forms _____

(g) Date of receipt of forms 2Q/2U/4/9LS, sent at your

request _____

(h) Initial tax claimed for current financial year (198) _____

(i) Adjustments made according to your reply to my letter,

ref. GH/54/GNR.23 _____

(j) Vehicular allowance estimated for current financial year

(198) _____

Date _____ Signed _____

Similar forms may be compiled for other Twitmarshes, though they must not be obviously bogus (the above example may be rather extreme; I leave it to readers to devise gambits of their own); it must be remembered that Twitmarshes, particularly tax men, are accustomed to sending out forms rather than receiving them, so that they may well be nonplussed. It is wise to make the form as official-looking as possible, and to give it a serial number. The best course, naturally, is to enlist the aid of someone who owns an amateur printing outfit.

Many forms — both from the Inland Revenue and from other official bodies — include sections which are left blank, with the brusque comment: *For official use only. Do not write in this space.* A very thin layer of candle grease smeared over this part of the form will make it quite impossible for the Twitmarsh to write on it with either a fountain pen or a ball-point, and after several abortive attempts he may well screw up the entire form in blind fury. If you have no candles to hand, a judicious amount of hair-cream or even oil will serve almost as well, though it is easier to detect and is therefore slightly less effective.

One very useful procedure is to put two tax departments, or two separate tax offices, in touch with each other. This is particularly applicable if you have moved house, say from Upper Doddington to Market Chickling. (It goes without saying that one should never notify the tax man of a move; let him find it out for himself.) When you hear from the tax inspector at

Market Chickling, where you have come to roost, write back to Upper Doddington. When you get a reply, write to Market Chickling, addressing it to Upper Doddington, and to Upper Doddington, addressing it to Market Chickling. You can then query the letter from Upper Doddington and send the inquiry to Market Chickling; as soon as you get an answer, mark it *For action, please,* and send it to whichever office has *not* replied. This can lead to interesting developments.

It may be claimed that this sort of gambit takes up as much of one's own time as the tax man's. True enough — but remember, you can do it when you like, whereas the tax man keeps strict hours (as short as possible) and will cope with nothing once he has departed for the golf course. So it is in a good cause.

Another useful tip is to send the tax man, out of the blue, a small cheque or postal order for which he hasn't asked, with a letter to the effect that you can't understand why this extra sum is being demanded, but of course you will pay as ordered. Make it just large enough to be unsafe to ignore (say £2.78). If it is returned, follow it up by asking why it was demanded in the first place (see F.L.s 1, 3, 4 and 8). When you get the next valid demand, deduct £2.78 and explain that this has already been paid (see F.L.s 3 and 4). There will then have to be a thorough check to see whether it has been paid, whether it has been refunded, or what the hell? If the cheque is not returned quickly, write and ask for it. Follow this up at regular intervals. I once had the great joy of sending a tax office a letter marked, in red, *Final*

Demand. My original cheque came back by return of post!

Another possibility is to spread alarm and despondency, using F.L.3. A courteous letter, asking whether it is true that Mr Basinby of the local tax office has queried the correspondence between yourself and the senior inspector, Mr Globberthwaite, can lead to mutual distrust between the two, which can act to your eventual advantage. But, of course, never say that Mr Basinby has actually made any comments at all; merely ask, making your letter as cryptic and sinister as possible. There is nothing illegal in this. The gambit is particularly worthwhile if you have managed to put two tax offices into futile correspondence with each other.

Finally — and this is vitally important, do remember it — make sure that you do nothing which is not strictly in accord with the law of the land, and make equally sure that your letters are courteous, innocent and even somewhat naïve. Twitmarshes do not usually have much sense of humour, but they must on no account be allowed to realize that they are being taken for a metaphorical ride. So be wary; do not overdo things. I repeat that some of the examples given here are rather near the limit (though in fact all are genuine, even if not all thought up by me). Never go too far.

Recently, the Inland Revenue has complained that its staff members are so overworked that unless something is done to alleviate their suffering, the entire tax system of the country may break down. What a wonderful thought!

A Note on
Languages

Most Twitmarshes are adept at murdering the English language. But English is not the only language spoken on earth. This leads on to some interesting possibilities which were, I admit, put into my mind when I read a newspaper account of how a Welsh Language fanatic had written to a local hospital in Welsh, and had been irritated to receive a reply in Hindi.

Many people receive official forms issued by Government departments and other Twitmarshes. These have to be filled in within a certain time, correctly, in full, and without any attempt at evasion. Failure to do so will involve the transgressor in a heavy fine. But — and this is the point — there is nothing in law to say that forms must be completed *in English*.

For instance, why not ask a linguistically minded colleague to fill it in in Greek, or even Icelandic? Hence the form will be returned as shown on pages 38–39.

For official use								

Claim FIS on this form

- When you have filled it in, send it to DHSS (FIS), Poulton-le-Fylde, Blackpool FY6 8NW (you can get a free stamped addressed envelope at a post office).
- Answer *every* question. Don't just put a dash. If you do your claim will be held up. And it may have to be sent back to you.
- Use BLOCK CAPITALS for all your answers.
- If you are a married couple (or living as man and wife) the man must be in full-time work.
- No one will be told what you put on this form.

1. Your name, etc. For a couple fill in details for both man and woman.

	Surname	Other names	Date of birth	National insurance number
Mr	ΠΑΡΑΣΚΕΥΟΠΣΥΛΟΣ	ΤΡΕΛΟΜΑΝΩΛΙΟΣ	34. 2.888	¥538456/721422/ΓΛ
Mrs/Miss	ΠΑΛΛΑΒΙΑΡΗ	ΑΦΡΟΣΥΝΗ	10.13.966	Ξ145942/376165/ΜΜ

Full address   ΜΑΝΤΕΙΟΝ ΤΩΝ ΔΕΛΦΩΝ 4562

ΠΑΠΑΤΡΕΧΑΓΗΡΕΒΕ   ΜΥΚΗΝΩΝ   Post code ΛΘΞΤ ΛΨΦ

- If either of you lives at a different address give it at question 11.

2. Do you have a FIS order book already? Answer YES or NO. ΝΑΙ

If YES what is the number of the book? ΛΩ93751427/ΚΠ _and_ what is the date on the last order? 10.10.1054

3. Your children's names etc

- Include only children who live with you and for whom you provide.
- Do *not* include any children the local council send to you as paid boarders.
- If you want to include in your claim any children who do *not* live with you write their names, present address, date of leaving home etc at question 11.

Child's surname	Other names	Date of birth	Name of school if child is over 16 and still at school full-time
ΓΕΡΟΝΙΚΟΛΑΟΥ	ΒΑΣΙΛΟΠΗΤΑ	14. 8.134	
ΜΑΛΕΒΡΑΣΑΚΗΣ	ΖΑΒΟΓΙΑΝΗΣ	14. 8.144	
ΝΥΧΡΕΡΗΔΙΑΔΗΣ	ΘΕΟΣΤΡΑΒΟΣ	14. 0.154	ΘΕΟΣΤΡΑΒΟΣ

4. Are you a lone parent? (single, widowed, separated or divorced, and not living with someone as husband and wife) Answer YES or NO. ΝΑΙ ΚΑΙ ΟΧΙ

If you are not the parent of the children, but are bringing them up alone, **put a cross** in this box. ☐

5. Are you getting child benefit?
Answer YES or NO ΝΑΙ
and who is it paid to? ΣΕ ΜΕΝΑ

If YES, how much each week? £0.13   *and* what is the number on the order book? Α1234567890

If NO, and you haven't claimed FIS before, please enclose birth certificates or other proof of age for each child listed. These will be sent back to you.

6. Do you work for an employer?
Answer YES or NO   Man ΟΧΙ   Woman ΝΑΙ

If YES, are you paid weekly or monthly? Say which ΜΕ ΤΗ ΒΑΟΜΑΛΑ

- If paid *weekly* fill in details for each of the last 5 weeks.
- If paid *monthly* fill in details for each of the last 2 months.
- Enclose any pay slips as proof, if you have them. If you don't (for example, if you have just started work) no need to delay claiming; we shall ask your employer for details (our enquiry will say that the information is required following an application for benefit: FIS will not be mentioned).

Your employer's FULL name and address	What is your job?	Pay week/month ending (fill in dates)	Hours worked in each week	Gross earnings *before* deductions (tax, national insurance etc). If **none**, write NONE.	
				Man	Woman
ΑΣΗΜΑΚΟΠΙΣΥΛΟΣ	ΙΕΡΕΙΑ ΚΑΙ ΕΤΑΙΡΑ	20. 9.81	4	£ . p	21⁹17 p
		27. 9.81	2	£ . p	476.35 p
		4.10.81	6	£ . p	300.03 p
		11.10.81	15	£ . p	£ 12.50 p
		18.10.81	27	£ . p	ΣΤΙΠΟΤΑ p
		25.10.81	10	£ . p	£0.10 p

Are these earnings what you normally get? Answer YES/NO ΝΑΙ ΚΑΙ ΟΧ If NO give details of any which are higher or lower than normal, saying why ΕΞΑΡΤΑΤΑΙ

How many hours a week do you *normally* work in this job? ΠΟΛΥ ΛΙΓΕΣ If you started your present job less than 5 weeks ago, give starting date

38

7. Are you self-employed?
Answer YES or NO — Man NAI Woman OXI — If YES, what is your trade or business? ΕΔΩΔΙΜΟΛΕΣΧΠΟΙΚΙΛΟΒΡΩΑΤΟΠΩΛΗΣ

What is your latest trading profit? £ 132.746.C4 — What period does this profit cover? 1C Μήνες — and how many hours a week do you normally work in this job? ΠΟΛΥ ΛΙΓΕΣ

● Enclose your latest profit and loss account if you have it. But don't delay claiming if you haven't.

8. Does either of you do any regular part-time work (less than 30 hours a week or less than 24 hours for lone parents) in addition to your full-time work? Answer YES or NO — Man OXI Woman OXI

If YES, fill in the details here for the last 5 weeks/2 months.

Your employers' name and address (if self-employed write SELF)	What is your job?	Pay week/month ending (fill in dates)	Hours worked in each week	Gross earnings *before* deductions Man		Woman	
				£ . p		£ . p	
				£ . p		£ . p	
				£ . p		£ . p	
				£ . p		£ . p	
				£ . p		£. . p	

9. Do you or your family have any other money coming in? Answer YES or NO NAI

If YES fill in the details here. Put in all your family's income, even if you think it may not count.

	How much each week	How often is it paid	Who is it paid to
Maintenance payments (for yourself and children), either voluntary or by court order (if they are not regular give details at question 11 instead)	£130 06 P	ΚΑΘΕΜΕΡΑ	Σ' ΕΜΕΝΑ
Pensions or benefits (other than child benefit – see question 5) Name of benefit ΕΠΙΔΟΜΑ ΑΝΩΤΑΤΗΣ ΕΠΙΛΟΣΗΣ Reference number ΤΕΜΠΕΛΙΑΣ	£25 ·10 P	ΚΑΘΕΜΗΝΑ	ΚΑΦΕΝΕΙΟ
Interest from savings or capital (fill in the gross amount *before* tax) Period covered χάθε δεκαπέντε μέρες	£421·74 P	ΤΟ ΧΡΟΝΟ	ΙΠΠΟΔΡΟΜΟ
Profit from boarders or sub-tenants Before you fill anything in here read the 'box' below	£58 .62 p	χάθε τόσο	ΤΑΒΕΡΝΑ
Any other income Description ΤΑ ΕΙΣΟΔΗΜΑΤΑ ΤΗΣ ΓΥΝΑΙΚΑΣ ΜΟΥ	£ ΟΛΑ p	ΑΜΕΣΩΣ	ΤΖΟΓΟ

Boarders and sub-tenants. Don't include your own family unless you're making a profit from them. Here's how to estimate your profit:

● **Boarders:** 20% (one-fifth) of the amount you charge each boarder is normally counted to be profit for you. For example, if you charge £15 a week, fill in £3 as profit. But this does not apply if the profit makes up a major part of your family income. In this case put the details in your answer to question 7 instead.

● **Sub-tenants:** If you let unfurnished, take away 50p a week from the rent you get. If you let furnished, take away £1. If you pay your tenants lighting and heating etc give details at question 11 instead.

---

10. Milk and vitamins are free for expectant mothers and children under school age in families getting FIS.

Do you already have any free milk token books? Answer YES or NO ΒΕΒΑΙΩΣ — If YES how many books? ΟΣΑ ΜΠΟΡΩ

and what are the dates on the last tokens in each book? ΑΥΡΙΑΝΗ ΣΥΝΗΘΩΣ Η ΤΟΥ ΕΠΟΜΕΝΟΥ ΜΗΝΑ

If NO are you waiting to hear the result of a claim for free milk? Answer YES or NO _____

Expectant mothers: when is your baby expected? Give date ΠΟΙΟΣ ΞΕΡΕΙ

11. Any other information which you think may help to decide your claim should be written here: ΑΝΩΤΑΤΟ ΥΨΟΣ ΣΠΑΤΑΛΗΣ ΚΑΙ ΚΑΛΟΠΕΡΑΣΗΣ ΣΥΝΔΥΑΣΜΕΝΟ ΜΕ ΕΞΑΙΡΕΤΙΚΗ ΕΠΙΔΟΣΗ ΣΤΙΣ ΓΥΝΑΙΚΕΣ ΣΤΟ ΚΡΑΣΙ ΚΑΙ ΣΤΗΝ ΠΡΕΖΑ

12. Post Office. If your claim is successful your FIS will be payable each week at a post office. Give the full name and address of the post office where you would like to be paid: ΤΡΙΑ ΜΙΛΙΑ ΑΝΑΤΟΛΙΚΑ ΑΠΟ ΤΟ ΑΚΡΩΤΗΡΙΟΝ ΤΟΥ ΣΟΥΝΙΟΥ

Declaration: In the case of a couple, both the man and woman must sign.

I/We declare that I/we have read the instructions on the form and to the best of my/our knowledge and belief the information given on this claim is true and complete. I/we claim family income supplement.

Warning: to give false information may result in prosecution.

Signatures:

Man _____ Woman _____ Date _____

You will be told the result of your claim as soon as possible

Also, Roman numerals can be substituted for the more conventional 1, 2, 3, 4. After all, the Romans themselves used them, even if it did land them in some mathematical difficulties (if you doubt me, try multiplying CLXXII by MCMLIX). But this is something of a giveaway, whereas an official receiving a form completed in, say, Serbo-Croat may not at once realize that the sender was born in Oldham and has never been to Yugoslavia in his life.

In a more extreme case it is permissible to use several languages, thereby filling in Part 1 of the form in Norwegian, Part 2 in Hungarian, Part 3 in Rumanian and Part 4 in Dutch, but this is recommended only when the earlier principles have been thoroughly worked out. Use a less familiar language when you can. Languages spoken everywhere in the country, such as Hindi, are no good at all, and French is not much better, since many people can speak it at least reasonably well. But how many Twitmarshes know Finnish, or are acquainted with anybody who does? Confronted by words such as *yksityiskohtaista* and *tähtijoukkomuuttujiski,*★ they will be at least temporarily baffled.

If these principles are widely applied, no doubt there will be an eventual change in the law; but for the moment the gambit is perfectly valid, and should be used whenever possible.

★Please don't ask me what these words mean. I haven't the faintest idea.

Official
Jargon

This may be the moment to pause and consider an important aspect of bureaucracy: its jargon. Sentences may be almost unbelievably convoluted (to my mind, the best of all was an Admiralty instruction issued during the war, concerning some mines which had to be stored the reverse way up for safety reasons: 'These mines must be stored with the bottom at the top. For clarification, the top of the container has been labelled *bottom*'). The following brief glossary is a general guide to what is meant.

Official reply	Actual meaning
Your letter has been carefully considered, and its contents noted.	I haven't looked at it.
I agree that action is perhaps desirable in this instance, and a full survey of the problem is being put in hand.	Nothing will be done.
I assure you that action in this instance will be taken as soon as possible.	Nothing will be done.

Official reply	*Actual meaning*
Action is, I agree, urgent, and will be taken in the near future.	Nothing will be done.
I fully appreciate the problem.	I couldn't care less.
I have every sympathy with your point of view.	What you think or don't think is a matter of total unconcern to me.
You are fully entitled to make your views known.	You can say and do what you like; nobody here will take a blind bit of notice.
I cannot agree with your point of view in this instance.	Of course you're right, but who cares?
Your complaint is being fully investigated.	Your letter has been put into the waste-paper basket.

Official reply	Actual meaning
Your complaint may have some validity in this particular instance, and will be investigated immediately.	Your letter has been put into the waste-paper basket.
A full and detailed reply will be sent to you in the near future, explaining all the circumstances of this case.	You'll be lucky!
There has, I agree, been a slight administrative error in this instance.	We've made a box of it, but we aren't letting on.
You will appreciate the very important complications in this problem.	I can't be bothered to look into it.
You will appreciate that this department is extremely busy, and is dealing with all matters outstanding with the minimum possible delay.	I'm playing golf at half past three.

Official reply	*Actual meaning*
I will be delighted to see you and to discuss this matter at your convenience.	If you try it, you'll find that I'm out.
I do not really feel that there is any useful purpose to be served in pursuing this matter further.	Get stuffed.
I will refer the whole matter to the appropriate department.	I will not refer anything to anybody; it will go into the waste-paper basket.
I assure you of our attention and consideration at all times.	Now I'll pull the other one!
The increase in tax/rates/ water rate/gas/electricity/ oil is unavoidable due to the current national financial situation.	I want another rise in my salary, and you are damned well going to pay for it.

BUREAUCRATS
HOW TO ANNOY THEM!

The Twit Percentage

In general, organizations and professions of all kinds — nationalized and otherwise — have members who are thoroughly sensible, members who are reasonable, members who are inclined to go off at a tangent, and twits. Obviously it is difficult to generalize, but the following table of Twit Percentages (T.P.) may be taken as an overall guide.

Organization	T.P.
Cricket Club committees	Inappreciable
Other sports club committees	3
Youth Club officials	7
Doctors, etc.	11
The police	12
Customs officials	27
Hospital boards	28
Motor licensing authorities (but see page 57)	44

Organization	T.P.
Political clubs	49
Licensing authorities	50
County Courts	51
The G.P.O.	57
The Church	61
The House of Commons	67
Planning authorities	70
Electricity boards	77
County Councils	79
British Rail	80
Gas boards	81
Education authorities	89

Organization	T.P.
Water boards	90
Parish Councils	91
Quangos	94
Psychiatrists	95
Social workers	97
Child psychiatrists	100

(Excluded from this table are the Trade Unions, which are above the law and cannot therefore be assessed, and the House of Lords, where the percentages — and even many of the noble Lords themselves — remain completely unknown.)

A full evaluation of the T.P. would take many pages,

and this is beyond the scope of the present preliminary study, so all that I can do is to add a few relevant notes. I regret that the subject is treated so incompletely; further researches are in hand, and will be published as soon as they become available.

THE POLICE

Very seriously, the police force as a whole does a splendid job, and the country would be in a state of even greater anarchy without them. Examples of genuine dedication and heroism are too numerous to mention. We are concerned here only with the remaining 12 per cent, accounting for the whole of the T.P. estimate. These are the 'rogue policemen' (R.P.s) who spend their time in bullying the private motorist.

The R.P. does not always reveal his true nature at a glance. He may look just like an ordinary, friendly, useful cop. It is also quite possible (according to a recent survey) that some policemen go through the R.P. stage for a limited period during their evolution, usually when they are anxious for promotion and have been passed over. The average R.P. is young, and may be one of two types: the disarming charmer ('I'm so sorry, sir, but did you know that this is a 30 m.p.h. limit, and you were doing a full 35?') and the blusterer ('You ought to know that you're exceeding the limit. I'll see your licence and insurance').

Drunken, incompetent and careless drivers deserve no sympathy at all. The menace of the R.P. is that he is out to catch the man (or woman) who is doing a few m.p.h. too many in a perfectly safe and deserted area. He has his own creed:

1 Know that every motorist thou mayst encounter is (a) drunk, (b) a liar, (c) easily cowed.

2 Keep thyself in hiding, with thy radar trap, the better to pounce upon thy fellow creatures.

3 Know that thou canst thyself break all traffic laws with impunity — provided there are no independent witnesses.

4 Thou shouldst never tackle a motorist for some trivial and harmless offence unless thou canst be sure that there are no awkward, unprejudiced witnesses. If thou shouldst be caught unawares, ensure that the witness is suitably frightened.

5 Thou must ensure that the motorist upon whom thou hast pounced does not carry a concealed tape recorder.

The first thing to establish, when faced with an R.P., is whether he has a valid case or not. If he has, there is not much you can do except keep silent and hope he will lose interest, so that he will go off and annoy someone else. If he hasn't, then ask for his warrant. If he is not carrying it, you can go on to the attack at once, particularly if you ask the name of his Chief Constable (which he probably won't know) and whether he is *au fait* with Section 17, Sub-section 8, of the Road Traffic Act (the numbers do not matter; invent them on the spur of the moment).

There are a few elementary ways to tell whether an officer is an R.P. or not. For example, he will give himself away if he tails you, and then dives into a garage ostensibly to refill with petrol, but actually comes straight out again in the hope that since you have seen the last of him, you will speed up. Another R.P. procedure is to tail a motorist very closely, inducing him to go faster and exceed a limit — at which moment the R.P. will zoom ahead, flash his 'Stop' signal, and pounce. If the victim has a passenger, however, it may be enough to look the R.P. squarely in the eye and say, 'Well, you were dangerously close, and to invite me to accelerate in order to put a safe distance between your car and mine is tantamount to incitement to break the law'. This has proved to be effective on more than one occasion. Finally, never plead guilty to a minor offence, and do not fall for the insinuation that you will therefore escape with an endorsement and a moderate fine, unless you really are at fault. The cunning of the R.P. knows no bounds — though let us repeat that in the police force as a whole he is fortunately a rare specimen, and some surveys have given the T.P. as well below 12.*

Quite apart from the R.P., there has recently been another sinister development: the emergence of the O.K.I., or Over-Keen Inspector, who makes a point of exhorting his merry men to nab as many motorists as possible. The O.K.I. does not seem to be common, and in most cases he keeps his name well out of the public eye, but occasionally he comes out into the open, and in so doing he does at least alert his potential victims.

For example, in August 1980 Chief Inspector Philip Newton, who heads traffic police in three divisions covering Nottingham and its suburbs, sent a circular to his sergeants in which he complained about the low frequency of 'bookings'. This, he said, was not at all satisfactory, and he added: 'I am alarmed at some of the figures shown in the monthly work returns for certain officers... I would suggest a minimum return of twenty offences a month would be indicative of an average police officer's work load. I look forward to a distinct improvement in the monthly figures.'

When the Press tried to question Mr Newton, he was (naturally) unavailable. However, the principle may well lead to a new unit of measurement, which should, I

---

*Some years ago, a notorious R.P. operating at Uckfield in Sussex was unwise enough to leave his parked car near a lamp-post in the main street. On returning, he found that his car had been securely chained to the lamp-post. However, this sort of revenge is naturally against the law, and cannot be condoned. I merely mention it.

suggest, be called the *newton* (not to be confused with the scientific newton, which is named after Sir Isaac rather than Chief Inspector Philip). We can even draw up a table, with each booking carrying a minimum score of 5 newtons: for catching a motorist doing more than 40 m.p.h. in a 30 m.p.h. limit, 10 newtons; for doing 45 m.p.h., 15 newtons, and so on. There could be a special award for any officer notching up 200 or more newtons in a calendar month.

It is not easy to tackle this new problem. The first step is probably to establish whether the traffic police in your area are or are not controlled by an O.K.I. Inspection of the court cases in the local paper will sometimes establish this, and if the presence of an O.K.I. is suspected a letter to the editor will do no harm. Check on the names of the police officers concerned in bringing pointless prosecutions, and draw up your own list, working out an appropriate scale in newtons. After a few months, contribute a second letter giving the results and the current league table. Further information can be obtained by carrying out a survey of the number of R.P.s operating in the area. Remember, however, that in some areas a normally friendly and harmless cop may be pressurized into behaving like an R.P., so there may well be extenuating circumstances.

TRAFFIC WARDENS
(About traffic wardens I will not write here, in view of the laws regulating the use of obscene language. I will say only that these wretched creatures, sub-human and de-

praved, are among the worst of all manifestations of modern civilization. Let us leave it at that.)

CUSTOMS OFFICIALS

(T.P. 27) are frequently maligned. Of course they are an infernal nuisance to everyone, but they are not often over-zealous these days, and generally speaking they are reasonable enough.

MOTOR LICENSING AUTHORITIES

(T.P. 44) do not usually give much trouble, except of course for the Swansea office, where there is a vast computer maintained by a staff about treble the number needed to operate the good old-fashioned system. Swansea is notorious. Getting a car licence takes weeks at best, months more normally; and trying to telephone is useless, as nobody ever bothers to answer. There is, however, one gambit which was employed some time ago by a friend of mine who was vainly awaiting a vital licence. After he had tried almost everything, and got nowhere, he selected a series of postcards and proceeded to send them daily, unstamped.

The first one read:

12 JUNE. First reminder. Please send my car licence at once.

The second, next day:

13 JUNE. Second reminder. Please send my car licence at once.

The third day:

14 JUNE.   Third reminder. Please send my car licence at once.

He eventually received it after card No. 26!

THE G.P.O.

With the G.P.O., quite apart from the ever-present problem of uncheckable telephone bills, there are occasional Twitmarshes who refuse to co-operate. I know of one specific case. A friend of mine had a number which was almost the same as that of the local hospital, so that he was plagued by callers asking for doctors, nurses, wards, etc. The G.P.O. refused to change his number; this, they said, would be too much of a problem. Finally my colleague adopted a novel ploy. He received a call at 1 a.m., and the conversation went as follows:

CALLER.   May I speak to Ward 5, please?

VICTIM.   *No.*

(A long, baffled pause.)

CALLER.   Why not?

VICTIM.   *Because you've been naughty.*

Two weeks of that, and the number was duly changed.

PLANNING AUTHORITIES

Next we come to planning authorities, where the T.P. is fairly high; 70 per cent may be an underestimate. The activities of Twitmarshes in this field are concentrated into two main spheres: (a) designing local road systems so as to cause the maximum of confusion, and (b) using their authority to block some completely innocent activity.

Let us deal first with point (a). The whole situation is exemplified by the city of Chichester in Sussex, which used to be a model of order; it is shaped essentially like an X, with the four main roads (named, not surprisingly, North Street, South Street, East Street and West Street) meeting at the famous ancient Cross. Admittedly the Cross has always been something of a hazard, but when the planners went to work they really surpassed themselves. First they created a pedestrian precinct, resurfacing the road at enormous cost and making it impossible to reach the centre of the city except on foot. (Within a matter of weeks the Gas Board had sent in their workmen to dig up much of the precinct. At the time of writing the hole was still there.) They then built a bypass which seems to wander as far afield as Grimsby in one direction and Plymouth in the other. Finally, they set up a system of one-way streets which defies all description.

A good opening gambit is to write to the Planning Officer, putting forward some constructive comments about the one-way system. Make them just sane enough to be taken seriously. You will probably get a rational reply, and your first letter can then be followed up with further suggestions. Before the Planning Officer realizes it, he will be embroiled in a long and quite futile correspondence. So far as Chichester is concerned, it may be that one could propose an elaborate subway beneath the level crossing at the end of South Street and then an airlift over the Cross.

True, this procedure does not often produce concrete results — and this is also the case when double yellow lines have been deliberately sited so as to cause as much inconvenience to the harassed motorist as possible — but it can be amusing. Moreover, it is occasionally possible to persuade the local paper to publish one's idea of a traffic revision, and nothing is more calculated than this to make a pompous Twitmarsh grind his teeth in rage.

So far as point (b) is concerned, the best plan is to expose the Twitmarsh's limitations in knowledge. For instance, there was the man who wanted to plant his garden with bushes of some kind; as it adjoined a road he had to obtain permission. It was refused. He sent in a second application, asking for permission to plant *Urtica diocia, Stellaria media* and *Taraxacum officinale*. It was granted, and he complied. *Urtica diocia* are stinging nettles, *Stellaria media* are chickweed, and *Taraxacum officinale* are dandelions. As he had official blessing, the Twitmarshes were in a difficult situation. When they received a new application for the original bushes, they granted it without a moment's hesitation.

COUNTY COUNCILS

These make up a mixed bag, mainly because they are inevitably made up chiefly of people who are too old to work, too young to work, or don't want to work at full-time jobs. We must therefore expect Twitmarshes in plenty (T.P. 79; some recent studies give 82). Various methods are available when dealing with them. There was, in particular, the man who applied for information about the rates increase to be demanded when he put up a new garage; the figure given was of the order of £20. He then wrote again, saying that he had had such a garage, but had now dismantled it and sold his car, so that his rates would have to go *down* by £20 — and they did.

In theory, County Councils collect the taxpayers' money to be used for the common good of the community. This is admirable, but in practice it doesn't always work; when money is obviously being thrown away, or used for the good of the Councillors themselves, action is possible. For example: in October 1980 (again! this seems to have been a good month for Twitmarshes), the Suffolk County Council took a long, hard look at their new £2,400,000 headquarters at St Edmunds House, Ipswich. They then decided to spend an extra £4,500 on pot plants to make it look nice. 'A lot of high technology has gone into designing these offices,' explained an anonymous Council architect. 'The plants are part of the design. They encourage people to work.'

In view of the current need for economy, some people would regard an expenditure of £4,500 on pot plants as being a little excessive, and there are even some taxpayers who would like to tell the Suffolk County Council what to do with their plants, pots and all. Unfortunately, such expenditure is hard to stop (and let it be said at once that Suffolk is very far from being the only offender).

One course is to write to the Chairman of the Council, enclosing a form and asking for various items of expenditure to be detailed. Look round carefully for a clear manifestation of waste, and single it out. You will, of course, have no reply, or at best an evasive acknowledgment. The next step is to write again, sending a duplicate to the local Press. When there is still no result, check on the regulations governing County Councils. With a certain number of signatories, the general public can convene an Extraordinary Council Meeting, which the Council is not empowered to refuse. Effective organization will, of course, ensure that the Press is present, and the first question to be raised will be the main point at issue — whether it be pot plants, the purchase of a new Rolls Royce for the Chairman, or anything else particularly relevant.

This has been tried on several occasions, and has been known to do some good. Basically, however, the only real remedy for a Council with a really high T.P. is to put up one's own candidates; this is horribly time-consuming, but has been done now and then. Some advantage may be gained by letting the Town Halls know that they are being closely watched, and asking why they are now employing forty extra staff, at vast salaries, to do the work formerly carried out quite competently by a mere dozen. But this is not really a satisfactory solution, and I have to admit that as yet nobody has come up with a complete answer. Suggestions will be welcomed, and will be incorporated in all future editions of this study.

BRITISH RAIL

(T.P. 80 per cent). Before nationalization, the British railway system was the best, the cleanest and also the cheapest in the whole world. Alas, times have changed, but one need not always submit meekly; remember the passenger revolts on the London Underground! The worst abuse is the emptiness of first-class compartments when there is 'standing room only' elsewhere. Some time ago, British Rail found a second-class passenger occupying a first-class seat, because there wasn't one anywhere else, and successfully claimed not only the difference, but the full fare. A few days later I was coming from Stoke-on-Trent to London on a train which was hopelessly crammed; together with others, I was standing forlornly in the corridor when an Inspector came along and demanded tickets. The conversation went as follows:

INSPECTOR.   Ticket, please.

ME.   I have it [I had!] but you're not getting it.

INSPECTOR.   You've got to give it up.

ME.   Sorry. I've paid for a seat, and I haven't got one.

INSPECTOR.   I'll put you out at the next station!

ME.   Good. That's Euston, and I'm going there anyway.

INSPECTOR.   I'll have the law on you!

ME.   Splendid. You call the police, while I call the Press.

INSPECTOR.   You won't get away with this!

ME.   Oh, no?

B - E

He went away, and came back shortly afterwards: 'I've got a seat for you, sir.' That took the wind out of my sails; I was in honour bound to surrender my ticket, but at least I ended the journey sitting down.

If all passengers in similar predicaments similarly refused to surrender their tickets, then British Rail would have to do something about it. There is no reason why they shouldn't. After all, they could make a handsome profit if they were run with even reasonable efficiency, and they cannot have any serious competition. It's a thought.

GAS BOARDS (T.P.81), ELECTRICITY BOARDS (77) and WATER BOARDS (90)

These can be lumped together. Water boards are perhaps the worst. The Southern Water Authority has been sending out bills of such striking magnitude that a Southern Water Action Group has been formed, and has already had a few successes. For example: in May 1980 the Authority set up a junket for the visit of the National Water Council, with lunch at over £18 a head and fifty-four bottles of wine for just sixty people, all of which was to come out of public funds. The Action Group charged in, and eventually Mr Arthur Smyth, Chairman of the Southern Water Authority, paid the bill, 'to save embarrassment'. At a meeting held in the same month, it was established without any shadow of a doubt that virtually all the 2,200 bills sent to ratepayers on the Isle of Wight were incorrect. The Action Group invited Mr Smyth to resign, but at the time of writing he is still firmly installed.

Then one occasionally receives a gas or electricity bill for £0.0p. This happened recently in Hampshire (or fairly recently; this particular bill was for £0.0s.0d, as it was just before we changed over from proper money to the Mickey Mouse money which doubled the cost of living 'at a stroke'). One can do one of two things: (a) Ignore it and await developments, or (b) send a cheque for £0.0p, subsequently claiming the value of a stamp (which can be deducted from the next bill). In the case cited above, gambit (a) was adopted. A summons was duly received, the case was scheduled at the local court — and it was a grave disappointment when, after the Press and other media had been alerted, the Electricity Board tumbled to what they were about to do, and withdrew the case at the eleventh hour.

QUANGO-HUNTING

This can be entertaining. Usually it is rather remote from everyday experience, though there was the recent case of a man who had quite a correspondence with the Race Relations Board after issuing a complaint about a shop in Kensington High Street which was advertising a white sale. (*En passant:* so far as the Sex Discrimination Act is concerned, nobody has ever fully explained the position of the Church re women clergy.) We may note, however, that one of the first decisive acts of the 1979 Conservative Government was to abolish the quango dealing exclusively with all matters pertaining to Hadrian's Wall. This was, I feel, a master-stroke in diplomacy, and may have far-reaching results.

DO-GOODERS

Finally, in this admittedly sketchy survey, we come to the do-gooders, of whom *social workers* are glaring examples. But, dim though they may be, with a T.P. of well over 90, they are essentially well-meaning, and do not concern us here. Neither do the *child psychiatrists* (T.P. 100 – a full house), even though as a class they have probably done more damage to the nation than anyone else. Just occasionally, however, one reads a story calculated to gladden the heart. Some time ago a boy of fifteen was brought before the courts, charged with firing a gun at a schoolmate; he was handed over to a child psychiatrist, who ruled that since the boy was under emotional strain the best course was to give him a new gun so that he could readjust. The gun was provided. And the fine, upstanding lad shot the psychiatrist in the leg.

BUREAUCRATS
HOW TO ANNOY THEM!

At Random

This will be a somewhat disjointed section, briefly discussing some points which did not seem to fit in anywhere else in this preliminary study. First, let us turn to a fairly new phenomenon: the *Bureaukraut.*

Bureaukrauts differ markedly from more conventional Twitmarshes. Consider, for instance, the Leicester bus episode of October 1980 (again we come back to that amazing month). A mentally handicapped woman was on a short bus journey with a pre-paid ticket. The fare had been put up to 16p. Her ticket was for 14p. Consternation! The driver radioed for help. The vehicle stopped, and bus inspectors swarmed aboard, uniforms polished and jackboots clicking. The passengers were turned out, the bus was diverted, and the luckless woman was held until social security officials turned up and paid the extra twopence. The Leicester City transport manager, Mr Geoffrey Hilditch, said that he 'fully supported' the bus staff.

I can only say that if I ever visit Leicester, I will studiously refrain from going on a bus.

Then there are officials of the London Electricity Board, who have a habit of disconnecting supplies to O.A.P.s if bills are late in being paid. During 1979 there was a total of 10,064 disconnections, including one concerning a diabetic who depended upon his refrigerator to store insulin, and another involving a mother with two babies who was in default by £15.82. These actions were defended by the usual anonymous spokesman who referred to the current economic situation.

We must face the fact that the only way to deal with a

Bureaukraut is to show him up for what he is, and letters to the Press are the best outlet; but to go further into matters of this sort would be too much of a digression from my main theme.

Returning to the more harmless officials, one can come up against *self-opinionated experts* on all sorts of subjects. It is on record that a local museum once exhibited a Roman coin bearing the head of Julius Cæsar and the date B.C.49. And there was certainly an urn on show with the cryptic inscription *Itisapis potitis andatino ne.* (It shouldn't take you long to work that one out!) But to apply the Fundamental Laws to people of this sort is frankly unkind, even though it can sometimes add to the gaiety of nations, and I would not recommend it.

Among miscellaneous pests there are *book clubs* who send out unwanted volumes, together with invoices, to be returned if not required. In many cases the recipient can't be bothered to do much about it, after which threatening letters start to arrive: 'Return these books immediately or else...' Possibly they have been mislaid – or the victim simply can't find enough paper and string to pack them up for return.

There is, however, one very useful gambit. Some months ago I was sent three large volumes dealing with the history of Brazil, in which I was not in the least interested; all I know about Brazil is that it is the country where the nuts come from. I waited for the first demand. When it came, I wrote back as follows:

Dear Sirs:

  Thank you for the books sent for storage in this Library. The storage charge is 50p per volume per week. The books have now been stored for a total of 4 weeks, making a preliminary charge of £6.0p. Your remittance by return of post will be appreciated.

I never heard another word!

RELIGIOUS PESTS can be dealt with easily enough provided that one never allows them to get even one foot inside the front door. I have tried several methods, all of which seem to work:

1   Greet him with: 'I'm sorry. I'm a Druid, and I'm a busy Druid. Good afternoon.'

2   'No, I haven't been reading the Bible lately. I really have no time to delve into science fiction. Good afternoon.'

3   'I'm sorry I can't entertain you myself, but I know that Dr Alonzo Schmidt, of 52 Mulberry Avenue, Wissington-on-the-Hill, is interested in your views and would be delighted to see you.' (As

there is no Dr Schmidt, and Wissington-on-the-Hill is at least fifteen miles away, a second visitation is unlikely.)

SPECIAL OFFERS. Have you ever had those cards offering you a sales bargain, or perhaps a cheap book, provided that you return the YES label attached? Collect them if you can — and send them on behalf of any Twitmarsh who is proving recalcitrant. It is almost certain to baffle him, and to involve him in pointless correspondence which will use up a pleasing amount of his time.

THE RECORDING DEVICE. It sometimes happens that when ringing the office of a civil servant or a nationalized industry — and this includes the Post Office — one is greeted by a recording device, which says in bland tones: 'This is Mr Upjohn's recording service. We regret that the office is at present closed. Please speak loudly and clearly, and leave your message following the short tone. . . bleeeeeep!' After several such experiences, the luckless caller may be forgiven for wanting to throw his telephone to the ground and stamp on it. This, however, does no good, and more subtle methods are recommended.

One course is to check up on the number of another Twitmarsh who has been giving trouble. Say that his number is Little Squelchpool 9191. On receiving the recorded message, say, in sepulchral tones: 'Please ring

Little Squelchpool 9191 between 1 and 2 p.m. tomorrow, Friday the 14th.' (The period between 1 and 2 p.m. is chosen because it is certain to be included in the Twitmarsh's extended lunch break.) If you have had a similarly recorded reply upon ringing Little Squelchpool 9191, leave a message of the same type, asking him to ring the first Twitmarsh between 5 and 6 p.m. Much confusion can thereupon be caused. But − and this is important − you must always leave the name of the Twitmarsh who is to be contacted. Otherwise, suspicion will be aroused at once.

I have once managed to put an official recording machine out of action. Following the usual short tone, I spoke, as instructed, loudly and clearly, as follows: 'This is for the attention of Mr Fobbage. Please may I speak to ... speak to ... speak to ... speak to ... speak to ...' and I rang gently off. I gather that engineers spent most of the following day dismantling the machine and trying to locate the fault!

Writing to
the Papers

Correspondence in the columns of the national or local Press can be fruitful if properly planned. Years ago, for instance, there was the famous article in a London daily about traffic control. When the first morning editions had been printed, and a number distributed, a sub-editor rang the editor and pointed out that (a) the article didn't quite make sense, (b) it ended with the words 'In this way the whole problem can be turned upside-down', and (c) the name of the author was R. Supward.

Much later, the august *Times* printed a letter from an indignant correspondent who wanted the game of chess to be banned on racialist grounds, inasmuch as it set white men up against black men.

Local papers can more frequently provide means of harassing Twitmarshes. A case in which I admit to having been involved occurred in Sussex around 1947. The local Parish Council was known to have a T.P. of well above average, and took serious notice of a letter in the *East Grinstead Observer* suggesting that the River Medway at Forest Row should be broadened and equipped with de luxe bathing machines, so that the village could be converted into a sort of Le Touquet. This was followed up in the next issue by objections from a non-existent sanitary engineer named W.C. Plummer, who said, quite correctly, that at Forest Row the Medway was about three feet wide and full of mud. Almost at once there was a flood of perfectly genuine letters.

'The Continental Sunday Must Not Come to Forest

Row' was one heading. Finally the Parish Council called a meeting, and discussed the whole project with owlish seriousness. The truth came out only with the publication of a final letter from another mythical resident, a Mrs U. Rynall. . .

Ministries, of course, are always good targets, and every department is stuffed with Twitmarshes. Generally they are too remote to be a nuisance, but they can be fun.* For example, what do you know about the regulations governing imported cucumbers?

In 1962 a Standing Committee (Cucumbers) was convened at Great Westminster House, London S.W.1. It was presided over by a judge, at public expense, and had one mission in life: to decide whether or not imported cucumbers should be stamped with the name of their country of origin. I wrote to the Committee, making some pertinent points.

---

*There are still echoes of the legendary harpsichord recitals given in Cairo, at the expense of the British Council, just before the Suez crisis of 1956; for some reason or other Colonel Nasser took no notice, and nationalized the Canal anyway. Another splendid British Council effort was to bring a Korean poetess to England and tour her round Fulham Gasworks. I can assure you that this actually happened!

Dear Sirs,

Unless all cucumbers are suitably marked, it seems that national prejudice will be bound to enter into the problem; a cucumber from, say, Czechoslovakia will be more conspicuous than one from a country with a shorter name, such as Java . . . I would recommend that cucumbers from the Soviet bloc be stamped in red, which will be a pleasant gesture; on the other hand, it might be considered offensive to stamp Chinese or Japanese cucumbers in yellow. There is also the problem of Oriental and Slavonic type-faces, and the ideal solution may be to have the name set in the language and alphabet of the country of origin, with a translation underneath. Italic type will not be suitable, and a bold Roman face is far better for cucumbers of ordinary size and texture.

I ended by expressing my regrets at my inability to attend the inquiry in person.

Mr G.L. Little, Secretary of the Committee, replied promptly and courteously, sending me a sheaf of material about cucumbers. I then asked about the sizes of the markings; should the lengths, etc., be given in Imperial units or metric? Mr Little's reply was again prompt. I reproduce it in full.

Office of the Standing Committee,
Great Westminster House,
Horseferry Road, London S.W.1.

MERCHANDISE MARKS ACT 1926.

Application for a Marking Order for Imported Raw Cucumbers, other than Gherkins.

Under the authority of the Statutory Instruments made under the Import Duties Act of 1958, fresh or chilled gherkins are now classified under sub-heading 07.01 (O) of the current Customs and Excise Tariff. Fresh or chilled cucumbers (other than gherkins) are classified under sub-heading 07.01 (D). In distinguishing between gherkins and cucumbers, account is taken of the botanical classification of the goods, but in cases of doubt the Commissioners of Customs & Excise are normally prepared to admit as gherkins goods which do not exceed 5'' in length, provided at the time of importation they are packed and invoiced as gherkins.

G.L. LITTLE,
Secretary.

Mr Little enclosed another wad of bumph dealing with cucumbers. For example, Mr F.N. Harrison, of the National Farmers Union, commented that 'the Union is quite convinced that the cucumbers should be marked with the country of origin on the "handle". This is the part of the cucumber which is not normally consumed.' Mr J.M. Wood, of the Parliamentary Committee at 63 Lincoln's Inn Fields, was worried that 'it would be necessary to be able to satisfy the Court about the origin of a cucumber in the event of a prosecution, and as we contend that this is highly improbable, the law would be brought into disrepute'.

I replied at once to Mr Little:

Dear Sir,

I have one further suggestion, which I make with some diffidence. Would it not be possible to mark the cucumbers in Esperanto? This would serve all purposes. Also, I feel that the question of units is vitally important. With regard to gherkins, I would recommend either giving the maximal length in both Imperial and metric, or else introducing a special unit to be known as the *gherk.* The only alternative would be to classify all goods as ghercumbers, which would be cumbersome. I note finally that the Fruit Importers' Association has raised the objection that it would be essential to stamp the cucumbers on both ends, as they (the cucumbers, not the Fruit Importers) are frequently cut in half. There should however be no difficulty in stamping them right through, and this could be done in small type during infancy, as the stamp would then grow with the gherkin (or cucumber).

Mr Little's reply this time was to send an even vaster wad of material, and to invite me to the public inquiry. I would have gone, but for the fact that the *Daily Mirror* somehow cottoned on and printed a light-hearted column headed

SAY IT WITH CUCUMBERS,

inferring that the Ministry was having its leg slightly stretched!

Last of all, in this admittedly brief study, what about the clerical Twitmarshes?

Again most of them are harmless, albeit humourless, but with the real extremists there is no reason not to apply at least some of the Fundamental Laws. In Northern Ireland, in 1967, there was a religious argument in the Portadown Town Council, with Protestants on one side of the fence and Roman Catholics on the other (I forget which was which), the point at issue being whether or not children should be allowed to use the swings in the public park on Sundays. The whole situation was clearly most interesting. Mrs Mary Hackett of Wylands Lodge, Belfast (who doesn't exist), published the following letter in the Province's leading daily, the *Belfast News-Letter:*

Sir:
   I have followed the controversy about Sunday swings for children with keen interest.

As a Christian, I am entirely opposed to the use of swings on God's Sabbath, and practising Christians with whom I have discussed the matter are in agreement.

There is, however, one further point upon which I am not clear. I have a pet budgerigar, which has a swing in its cage. I have made a practice of disconnecting the swing each Saturday night and not putting it back into use until Monday morning. Is this in accord with Christian principle?

And that was where the fun started. To the best of my knowledge and belief all the following letters, which poured in for weeks, were perfectly genuine. For example:

Sir:

It seems to me that this is a problem of considerable importance, as Darwin has shown that there is really little difference between animals and man, and the Holy Book itself states, 'Consider the birds of the air.'

After all, Sunday is Sunday whether one is animal or human, and one cannot allow domesticated animals to set a bad example to our children; wild animals, however, cannot be blamed, as this is purely a man-made problem — the denizens of the forest, swinging through the trees, cannot be compared with a budgie in its cage.

Mrs Hackett's excellent example should be a lesson to all those who seek to desecrate God's Sabbath, and to those who were in doubt as to how far the alarming trend in moral laxity should be allowed to develop.

M.J. Metcalfe.

Sir:

To add further comment to the dispute concerning the swings in Portadown, I suggest that it is the responsibility of parents, not the Town Council, to decide whether or not they will allow their children to swing on Sundays.

Moreover, I must protest strongly at the incomprehensible reasoning of the lady who disconnects the swing in her budgie's cage every Saturday. Does she really believe that her action is leading her budgie's soul on the path to Heaven? And does she also take it to church with her?

S.C. Day.

Sir:

I vehemently oppose Mary Hackett's suggestion of the removal of her budgerigar's swing on a Sunday. I regard this as an encroachment into our British liberty. We, too, possess a budgie to which my dear wife is devoted. Many a Sunday we have watched his antics in idle tranquillity, obtaining from his pleasure a delight of our own.

P. Field.

Sir:

The answer to Mrs. Hackett is — it all depends upon whether the budgerigar is a Protestant or a Roman Catholic bird. It is commonly thought that we Protestants believe that all Roman Catholic budgerigars go to hell by predestination. We do not think that at all. We believe that all Papists, budgerigar or human, go to hell on their merits.

M. Malcolm McKee.★

Sir:

Mrs Hackett may be assured that her attitude is entirely Christian. What I am worried about are the monkeys and apes at the Zoo. If they are, as Darwin has told us, relatives, then they should not swing on Sundays.

S.W. Sands.

★I am not too sure about the sincerity of this one!

> *Sir:*
>
> *How lucky we are that Mrs Hackett's budgie does not join the noisy feathered battalions that foul and damage our clothes and buildings. I already have the message.*
>
> *H. Gibson*

> *Sir:*
>
> *All creatures should obey the Ten Commandments. I habitually read the Bible to my St. Bernard each Sunday morning.*
>
> *William Mahoney.*

By now the broadcasting media were interested, and the story was featured on the television news. The episode was ended by a Mr William Quinn, who meanspiritedly published a letter pointing out that many people were perhaps taking the whole matter a little too much to heart. The correspondence died; whether the Town Councillors ever 'got the message', like Mr Gibson, I do not know — but for a brief period the Portadown budgerigar was probably the most famous bird in all Ulster.

Epilogue

It must again be stressed that this slim volume is nothing more than a preliminary study. Much remains to be done, and further researches are needed before a concentrated campaign can become possible. But if the Fundamental Laws are rigorously applied, they can do a great deal of good.

Twitmarshes, as a class, complain that they are underpaid, overworked, and crippled by inflation. This, alas, is not actually the case; but if we could make it so, then how wonderful life would become! If the F.L.s are used consistently throughout the country it might even lead to a general strike of civil servants, and this would be the best thing possible. If it ever came to pass, the rest of us would be able to get on with some real work.

So — don't delay. Make a New Year's or even a New Month's resolution. WRITE TO YOUR TAX INSPECTOR TODAY. And the best of British luck!

Index

Swansea, licensing authority (cars) at, inertia of, 57—8

Tähtijoukkomuuttujiski, 40
Taraxacum officinal, see Dandelions
Tax Avoidance experts, 27
Taxman, short working day of, 33
Telephone service, 14
Telephones, changing numbers of, methods of, 58
Thompson, Mr and Mrs, 15
Town Halls, methods of supervising, 62
Trade Unions, status of, 27, 51
Traffic Wardens *(entry censored)*
Twit Percentage (T.P.), 47—54; table of, 49—51
Twitmarsh, Mr, 9, 10
Twitmarshes, 9, 10, 14, 15, 16,

18, 21, 22, 34, 58, 60, 71, 73, 87; clerical, 81

Uckfield, episode at, 55*n*
Underground system, London, 63
Urtica diocia, see Stinging nettles

V.A.T. men, characters of, 26

White sale, Kensington High Street at, report of, 65
Whitmarsh, Mr K., *see* Twitmarsh, Mr
Whitty, Miss (North Thames Gas Board), 10, 12, 13

YES, 71
Yksityiskohtäista, 40

Zimbabwe, *see* Rhodesia